HOW-TO LIBRARY

BUILDING SANDCASTLES

By Dana Meachen Rau
Illustrated by Kathleen Petelinsek

CHERRY LAKE PUBLISHING • ANN ARBOR, MICHIGAN

CHERRY
LAKE
Publishing

Published in the United States of America by Cherry Lake Publishing
Ann Arbor, Michigan
www.cherrylakepublishing.com

Content Adviser: Dr. Julia L. Hovanec, Professor of Art Education,
Kutztown University, Kutztown, Pennsylvania

Photo Credits: Page 4, ©wavebreakmedia ltd/Shutterstock, Inc.; page 5,
©Fabiofersa/Dreamstime.com; page 6, ©YuriyZhuravov/Shutterstock, Inc.;
page 7, ©Ruforester/Dreamstime.com; page 11, ©Kmiragaya/Dreamstime.
com; page 29, ©Dana Meachen Rau; page 32, ©Tania McNaboe

Library of Congress Cataloging-in-Publication Data
Rau, Dana Meachen, 1971–
  Building sandcastles / by Dana Meachen Rau.
    p. cm. — (How-to library. Crafts)
  Includes bibliographical references and index.
  ISBN 978-1-61080-468-4 (lib. bdg.) —
  ISBN 978-1-61080-555-1 (e-book) — ISBN 978-1-61080-642-8 (pbk.)
1. Sand craft—Juvenile literature. 2. Sandcastles—Juvenile literature. I. Title.
  TT865.R38 2013
  736'.96—dc23   2012014012

Cherry Lake Publishing would like to acknowledge the work
of The Partnership for 21st Century Skills. Please visit
www.21stcenturyskills.org for more information.

Printed in the United States of America
Corporate Graphics Inc.
July 2012
CLFA11

The author would like to thank Ed Jarrett, the Guinness
World Record holder for the world's tallest sandcastle, for
sharing his knowledge of and enthusiasm for sand building.

A NOTE TO ADULTS:
Please review the instructions for these craft projects before your children make them. Be sure to help them with any crafts you do not think they can safely conduct on their own.

A NOTE TO KIDS:
Be sure to ask an adult for help with these craft activities when you need it. Always put your safety first!

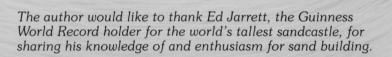

HOW-TO LIBRARY

TABLE OF CONTENTS

A Day at the Beach

What do you like to do at the beach?

Pack up the car for a day at the beach. Perhaps you like to go to the ocean. Or maybe you swim at a lake. You'll need a lot of supplies for all of the fun and sun. Be sure to bring towels, an umbrella, and sunscreen. Don't forget the buckets and shovels.

Beaches at oceans and lakes are great places to play in the sand. You can spend hours planning, molding, and carving sand into sculptures. Choose a flat work site to start building on. The best spot should be close to the water. This makes it easy for you to get water when you need it. If you are at the ocean, look for the high tide line. If the tide is going out, the wet sand on the beach will be useful for building. But if the tide is coming in, be sure to place your sand sculpture far enough away that the waves won't knock it down.

What kind of sand sculpture will you make? Use your imagination to form sand into amazing designs.

PACK YOUR BAGS!
Make a checklist as you pack for the beach. Then you won't end up on the sand without an important tool for your sandcastle.

Imagine what you can make!

Why Sand Sticks

Dry sand runs through your fingers.

Have you ever tried to make a sandcastle out of dry sand? You probably discovered that it doesn't keep its shape. It just falls apart.

Sand is made up of lots and lots of tiny grains. If you hold a handful of dry sand, the grains fall through your fingers. But wet sand clumps together. That's because water helps the grains of sand stick together.

Scientists have studied why this happens. Water forms little bands in the spaces between the grains of sand. Scientists call these "liquid bridges." The sand no longer acts as single grains. The grains move together as a clump instead.

The sand on a beach's surface is not the best for building. Surface sand has been raked and walked on. If you are at the ocean, it has also been worn and **eroded** by ocean waves. This makes the grains smooth. You need sand grains that are still **irregular** in shape. So you have to dig a little deeper to the sand underneath.

WORKING TOGETHER
Ask friends and family to join you in making a sand sculpture. Not only will the project go faster, but it will also be more fun. Many creative minds working on a project make it even better.

Wet sand has a soft, sticky texture.

Basic Tools

You may have all the tools you need in your house, garage, or basement already. Your hands are the best tools for digging, scooping, packing, and smoothing out sand.

- *Shovels*—You'll need large and small shovels, depending on how much sand you plan to dig.
- *Buckets*—Bring along buckets in a variety of sizes to carry water and to mix sand and water together.
- *Molds*—Molds will give your sand shape. You can use traditional molds, such as buckets and bowls, by filling them up with wet sand and flipping them over. But this method can make your tower topple unless you poke holes in the bottom of the container to loosen the **suction**.

Bottomless buckets can help you build much stronger structures. You can make **cylinder** molds by cutting off the bottoms of plastic buckets, containers, and cups. For a really big cylinder, use a plastic trash can. Plastic-coated cardboard milk cartons can make rectangular blocks. Do not cut the bottom off a container yourself! Always have an adult cut it for you. He or she will need to use a box cutter, kitchen shears, or other sharp tool that can be very dangerous.

You can use scraps of roofing paper to make molds in any shape. Roofing paper is a sturdy but **flexible** material. You can easily cut it to any height with scissors, roll it into a tube shape, and secure it with duct tape. If you are making a

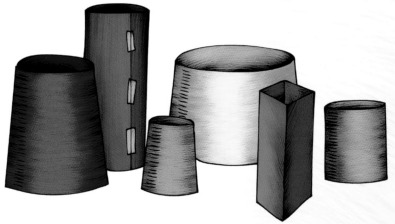

mold up to about 12 inches (30.5 centimeters) wide, roll the paper in a single layer. If you are making a larger cylinder, you'll need to wrap the paper around a few times to create multiple layers to support the sand.

- *Carving and shaping tools*—A cake spatula used for spreading frosting is good for smoothing out sand. A paint scraper has a square tip to help you make stairs. Use plastic forks, knives, and spoons to add details and scoop out small areas. Draw lines and designs with a wooden skewer or toothpick. Funnels, cookie cutters, and other kitchen tools can shape sand, too. While you are carving, blow off loose sand with a drinking straw. Brush away fallen sand with an old paintbrush.
- *Decorations*—Keep your decorations natural. Feathers, shells, seaweed, and driftwood are great decorations to use at the ocean. If you are near a lake, use pebbles, pinecones, and other natural items you find in the area.

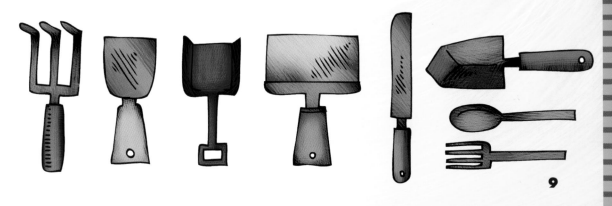

Firm Foundation

Your castle needs a firm foundation. Draw the "footprint" of your structure in the sand. Make the area a little bigger than you think you'll need. Then scrape off the surface sand with a shovel so that you have a clear, flat area of moist sand to start building on.

Mixing Your Materials

Dig a deep hole next to your foundation. You may actually reach water if you dig deep enough. If not, add water to the sand in the hole. Keep a bucket of water nearby for when you need to add more. Mix the sand and water together in this mixing hole.

You can also mix sand and water in a bucket. Whether you use a mixing hole or a mixing bucket, it's important to mix the sand and water before you start building. It helps the grains stick together.

When you scoop out handfuls of sand from the hole or bucket, pack it in your hands so that it is moist and moldable, but not soupy. Some sandcastle experts call this "patty-cake" sand.

NO SHORTCUTS
You may think it would be faster to make a mound by shoveling sand into a pile and pouring water over it. But this won't give you a sturdy structure. The sand won't absorb the water past a certain level. Your sculpture will crumble when you try to carve it.

Scrape off the surface sand to reach the sand underneath.

Building Bases and Mounds

If you want to make a base for your structure, scoop sand out of the mixing bucket or hole. Place it on the foundation and pat it down with your hands. Continue adding more handfuls of sand and slapping your hands all over the surface. This will **compress** the sand, get the air out, and help the water drain out the bottom. The grains will stick together into a solid base. Scrape across it with a shovel or spatula to flatten the surface. Now you can start to build your structure on top of it.

You can also use this method to make a larger mound. Just keep adding scoopfuls of sand and patting them down until you reach the height you want.

Working with Molds

Sand sticks best when you can pour water into it from the top. That way, water can absorb down through all of the grains and drain out the bottom. You can pack it down to get all of the water out. That is why you need a mold that is open on both ends.

Filling Molds

Place your empty mold on your foundation or base. Scoop in a few inches of sand. Then add some water.

If you have a large mold, you'll need a partner. Climb into the top of the mold. Have your friend add sand and water. Then dance around on the sand in the mold. Ed Jarrett, the Guinness World Record holder for the world's tallest sandcastle, calls this method "squishy feet." Stamping on the sand packs it down and gets out the air. The sand should be the **consistency** of toothpaste. To be safe, you may want to have your friend pack some dry sand around the base of the mold to help keep it steady.

Stamp down the sand in a large mold with your feet.

If you have a small mold, try the "squishy fingers" method. Pound down the sand in the mold by "stamping" on the surface with your fingers like little feet.

No matter how big your mold is, keep adding more sand. Then add more water and let it soak in until it puddles on the top. Stamp some more. Continue until you have filled the mold.

Removing Molds

If you used roofing paper, pull off the duct tape and unwrap your structure. If you used a bottomless bucket, carefully lift it up and off. You can also cut molds in half and secure them with duct tape. Then just peel off the tape and take the mold off both sides when you are ready to remove it.

A bucket or cup cut in half will be easier to remove.

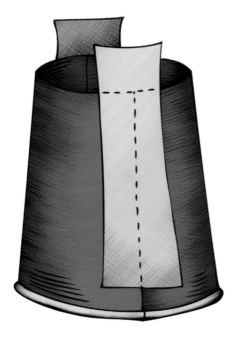

GIVE IT TIME
If you are making a very large structure, you need to leave it in the mold long enough for the water to drain down. Let it sit for a few hours, or even overnight, before you remove the mold. You only need to wait a few minutes if you are using a small mold.

Carving Details

Always start working at the top and move downward.

After you've unmolded your sand structure, you can carve out the details. Clumps of sand will fall off as you carve. You don't want to mess up the lower levels of your sculpture. So always carve from the top down. Don't remove your molds all at once if they are stacked on top of each other. Remove the top one and carve the sand before you remove the next one.

Draw on the sand first to plan where to carve. Then scrape away a little sand at a time. Blow loose sand away with a straw.

To make windows and doors, scoop out the sand on the surface with a plastic spoon. Smooth out the edges with a spatula. To make stairs,

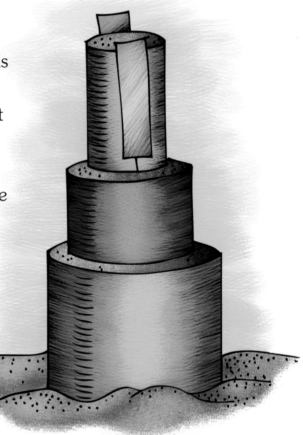

14

Carve in first, then down when making stairs.

2nd ↓

←1st

carve into the sand from the side, then down from the top to cut out a wedge shape.

To make evenly spaced lines, use a garden hand fork or a plastic fork. Experiment with different tools to get different effects. Use a paintbrush to clean up fallen sand when you are done.

You may need to go back to add details to the top after you've reached the bottom. To protect your work, carefully wrap a trash bag around the areas you've already carved.

REBUILD AND REPAIR

Work slowly and carefully. If you knock off some sand by mistake, make some patty-cake sand. Lift and gently press it to the area where you need it. Use your hands as a mold and hold it in place. You may have to hold it for a few minutes until the sand sets. Then wait about half an hour before you start carving it again.

Haunted Hill

If your sand and water mixture is soupy and drippy, you have made drizzling sand. This isn't good sand to make a firm foundation, base, or mound for carving. But it is good for making drip castles. Use this method to make a spooky castle on a hill.

Materials

Buckets and shovels
Paint scraper
Seaweed

Let the wet sand drip slowly from your hand.

Steps

1. Prepare your area by making a firm foundation and setting up a mixing hole or bucket (*see pages 10–11*).

2. Build up a mound with handfuls of patty-cake sand. It can look rough and irregular. This will be your mountain.

3. Mix up sand and water so that it is oozy and drips out of your fingers if you squeeze it. Hold your hand over the top of the mound and let the drizzling sand drip from your fist into little mounds on your foundation.

Create a long winding staircase up to your castle.

4. Make a bunch of these drippy-looking castles in different sizes and heights all around the top of your mound.
5. Using the paint scraper, carve stairs from the top winding down to the base of your mountain.
6. Place seaweed around the castles and hang it from some of the mountain cliffs to add to the spooky mood.

Classical Temple

Look at photographs of castles, temples, and other structures from ancient history. They might inspire you to build a wonder of the world in sand.

Materials

Buckets and shovels
5-gallon (19 liter)
  bottomless bucket
Spatula
Wooden skewer
Plastic spoon

Plastic fork
Drinking straw
Paintbrush
Paint scraper
Pruning shears
Dry grasses or twigs

Steps lead up to this round columned structure.

Steps

1. Prepare your area by making a firm foundation and setting up a mixing hole or bucket (*see pages 10–11*).
2. Build up a base wider than your mold with handfuls of patty-cake sand. Smooth the top flat with the spatula.

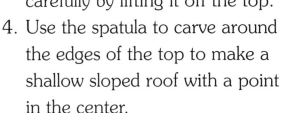

3. Fill your bottomless bucket mold as described on pages 12–13. Let it sit for about half an hour to let the water drain out. Remove the bucket carefully by lifting it off the top.

4. Use the spatula to carve around the edges of the top to make a shallow sloped roof with a point in the center.

Scoop out the sand with a spoon.

5. Use the skewer to draw lines all around the structure from top to bottom to mark where your columns will go.

6. Scoop out the sand between the columns with the plastic spoon. Smooth out the sand with the back of the spoon.

7. Draw stripes on the columns by running the fork from top to bottom on each column. Blow away extra sand with the straw. Use a paintbrush to brush away the extra sand around the base.

8. Carve into the base with the paint scraper to make a ledge all around the temple. Smooth it out with the spatula. Carve a second ledge around the first and smooth it out.

9. Use pruning shears to cut dry sea grasses or twigs into short lengths. Arrange them on the roof of the temple coming out from the center.

Mini Modern City

How big will you make your city?

Design your own city, complete with skyscrapers and streets filled with cars.

Materials

Orange juice or milk carton molds

Buckets and shovels

Wooden skewer

Plastic knife

Drinking straw

Paintbrush

Toy cars

Steps

1. Prepare your molds before you go to the beach. Have an adult cut the tops and bottoms off orange juice or milk cartons, and clean them well.

2. Prepare your area by making a firm foundation and setting up a mixing hole or bucket (*see pages 10–11*).

3. Use the skewer to draw a **grid** on the foundation to plan where you want to place your skyscrapers and streets.

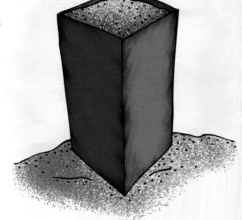

4. Place a mold where you want to build a skyscraper. Fill your mold as described on pages 12–13. Let it sit for a few minutes before pulling off the mold. Repeat this step to place buildings along your city streets.

Fill your open cartons to the top to make your skyscrapers.

5. Use the plastic knife to carve windows into the buildings. Blow off extra sand with a straw.

6. Brush extra sand off the streets with a paintbrush.

7. Place toy cars and other decorations to create a busy, bustling city.

Castle Tower

Use a large cylinder mold to make a castle tower. If you like to think big, use a trash can or roofing paper. Use a large bucket if you want to work on a smaller scale.

Materials

Large cylinder mold

4 empty 1-liter soda bottles

Buckets and shovels

Spatula

Plastic knife and spoon

Wooden skewer

Drinking straw

Paintbrush

Piece of bark

Steps

1. Prepare your molds before you go to the beach. If you are using roofing paper, cut it to size. Have an adult cut the tops and bottoms off some soda bottles to make small cylinder molds.

2. Prepare your area by making a firm foundation and setting up a mixing hole or bucket (*see pages 10–11*).

3. Place the large mold in the center. Fill it as described on pages 12–13. Since it is a large mold, you will need to let it sit for an hour or so. Then lift or unwrap the mold.

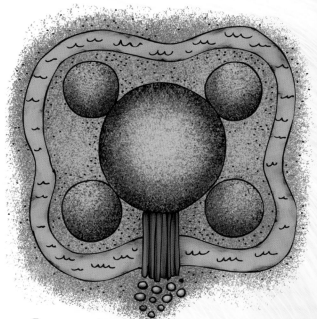

Place the smaller towers around the center one as shown in this view from above.

4. Place the four small cylinder molds around the center tower and fill them. Keep these molds in place while you carve the larger piece.

5. Carve your center tower from the top down. Carve battlements around the top with the spatula. Carve out thin windows with the plastic knife. Use the plastic spoon to scoop out some sand near the base to make a large doorway. Use the skewer to draw lines like blocks of stone all over the structure. Blow away extra sand with the straw. Brush extra sand from the base with the paintbrush.

6. Remove the small cylinder molds. Carve these smaller towers with windows and stone blocks like the larger tower.

7. Dig a moat around the castle and fill it with water. Place a piece of bark as a drawbridge to your doorway.

Sand Sentry

Now that you have a castle, you need someone to guard it! It is important to work from the top to the bottom and only take off one mold at a time. That way, you won't mess up the lower parts of your structure while you work.

Materials

Buckets and shovels
5-gallon (19 l) bucket mold
Large bucket mold
Small bucket mold
Wooden skewer
Spatula, plastic spoon, fork,
    knife, and other carving tools
Drinking straw
Paintbrush
Seashells and pebbles

Steps

1. Look at pictures of knights and armor before you go to the beach. Draw a sketch to help you decide what types of molds you need to make knight shapes out of sand.

2. Prepare your area by making a firm foundation and setting up a mixing hole or bucket (*see pages 10–11*).

3. Place the 5-gallon (19 l) bucket mold down first and fill it as described on pages 12–13. Do not remove it.

4. Place the middle-size mold on top of the flat surface of the first mold and fill it.

5. Finally, place the smallest mold on top and fill it.

6. Pull off the top mold. Use a skewer to draw your design onto the sand. Then carve the head of your knight with your spatula and plastic tools.

7. Remove the second mold to carve the top part of the knight's body.

8. Finally, remove the bottom mold. Carve the knight's legs and other details.

9. Add some patty-cake sand for feet. Carve them to look like boots.

10. Clean up your knight by blowing and brushing away extra sand with the straw and paintbrush. Add seashells, pebbles, or other natural jewels onto his armor or sword.

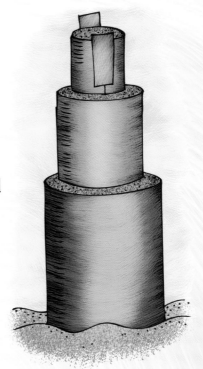

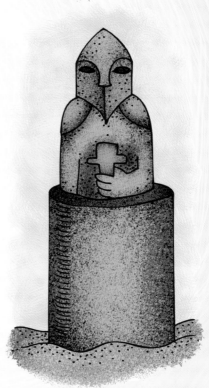

Always start carving from the top and work your way to the bottom.

Sand Maze

On the grounds of some castles, people enjoy walking and exploring mazes made of green hedge bushes. Create a winding path of sand with this swirly design.

Materials

String, at least 48 inches (122 centimeters) long

Shovel

Stick

Shells or pebbles

Steps

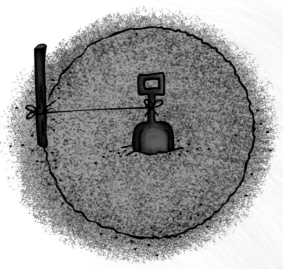

1. Find a flat area in the sand at least 8 feet (2.4 m) wide.

2. Tie the string onto a shovel and stick it into the center of your space. Tie a stick on the string about 12 inches (30.5 cm) from the shovel. Drag the stick on the sand around the shovel to make a circle.

3. Untie the stick and retie it 2 feet (0.6 m) from the shovel. Drag it around the center to make another circle.

4. Make circles around the center point at 3 feet and 4 feet (0.9 and 1.2 m). This creates a target shape.

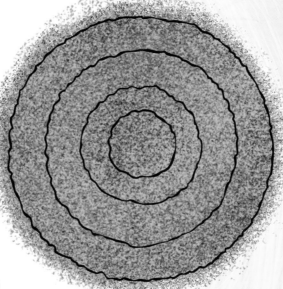

Use a shovel, string, and stick to draw sand circles.

5. Dig out the innermost circle with your hands. Push the sand along the edges and pat it flat to make a shallow space. This will be the center of your maze.

6. Along the lines of the other three circles, dig a path wide enough for walking and push the sand up along the sides.

7. Decide where you will enter your maze and extend the outer path out. Walk the outer circle until you almost reach the starting point. This is where you'll make your first turn. Place some sand to end the outer path. Then make a pathway to connect the outer circle to the next circle.

8. Now walk in the opposite direction around this circle. When you almost reach the spot where you started, block your path with sand. Then make a pathway between this circle and the next one.

9. Again, walk in the opposite direction until you almost reach your starting point. Connect this circle with the inner hole.

10. Smooth out the areas of mounded sand between the paths. Dot the sides of the walkway with shells or pebbles.

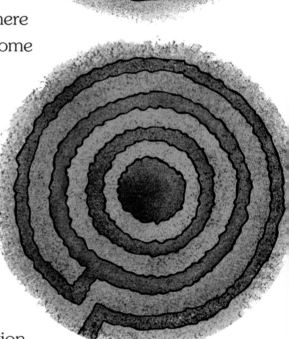

Connect each circle to the next with short pathways.

Practice and Experiment

Some sandcastle builders enter competitions on beaches all over the world. Competitors try to build high castles or ones with a lot of arches and windows. They try to create sculptures unlike anything anyone has ever seen.

If a sandcastle competition comes to your area, check it out. Watch how the experts build castles. Learn from their techniques. Maybe set up a sandcastle competition of your own with your friends on a hot summer day.

Remember that even experts make mistakes. Castles crash. Carvings crumble. Towers tumble. Keep trying if you get frustrated.

There are lots of ways to build a sandcastle. Experiment with different methods. Sometimes you can even turn mistakes into something great! The more you practice, the better you'll get at building amazing sculptures.

There's no limit to what you can create with sand.

Glossary

absorb (ab-ZORB) to soak up

compress (kuhm-PRESS) to flatten something into a smaller space

consistency (kuhn-SIS-tuhn-see) the thickness of a substance

cylinder (SIL-uhn-dur) a three-dimensional shape with two circular ends

eroded (i-RODE-id) worn away by wind, water, or other means

flexible (FLEK-suh-buhl) able to bend

grid (GRID) a pattern of crossed parallel lines

irregular (i-REG-yuh-lur) uneven in shape

suction (SUHK-shuhn) a force like a vacuum in a space with no air

For More Information

Books

Chapman, Gillian. *Making Art with Sand and Earth*. New York: PowerKids Press, 2008.

Gillman, Claire. *The Kids' Summer Fun Book*. Hauppauge, NY: Barron's, 2011.

Prager, Ellen J. *Sand*. Washington, DC: National Geographic Society, 2006.

Wierenga, Lucinda. *Sandcastles Made Simple*. New York: Stewart, Tabori & Chang, 2005.

Web Sites

Sand Castle Central

www.sandcastlecentral.com

Learn more about sandcastle building with these helpful tips and lessons.

Travel Channel: Sand Masters

www.travelchannel.com/tv-shows/sand-masters

Watch videos of master sand sculptors at work.

The World's Tallest Sandcastle

http://jarrettscastle.com

Check out photos and videos of the world's tallest sandcastle.

Index

About the Author

Dana Meachen Rau is the author of more than 300 books for children on many topics, including science, history, cooking, and crafts. She creates, experiments, researches, and writes from her home office in Burlington, Connecticut.